MW01265334

VALUE BIOGRAPHIES

COURAGE
The Story of
HARRIET TUBMAN

CHRISTA KELLY

childsworld.com

Published by The Child's World®
800-599-READ · www.childsworld.com

Copyright © 2026 by The Child's World®
All rights reserved. No part of this book may be
reproduced or utilized in any form or by any means
without written permission from the publisher.

Photography Credits
Photographs ©: Benjamin F. Powelson/Library of
Congress, cover, 1, 7, 11 (top); Shutterstock Images, 4–5, 6,
10, 11 (bottom), 13; Harvey B. Lindsley/Library of Congress,
9; Red Line Editorial, 15; Bettmann/Getty Images, 17, 20;
Chip Somodevilla/Getty Images News/Getty Images, 19;
Design element from Benjamin F. Powelson/Library of
Congress

ISBN Information
9781503871205 (Reinforced Library Binding)
9781503872547 (Portable Document Format)
9781503873780 (Online Multi-user eBook)
9781503875029 (Electronic Publication)

LCCN 2024950390

Printed in the United States of America

Christa Kelly is an author and editor
from Minnesota. She lives with her
wife, Clare, and their two cats, Casey
and Honey Cheddar.

TABLE OF CONTENTS

FINDING FREEDOM

Harriet Tubman had her eyes on the sky. She was following the North Star. She had been walking for hours. Every night, she followed the star until sunrise. Then she hid and waited for nightfall. If she got caught, she might be beaten or killed. But the pull of freedom gave her the courage to continue north.

After weeks of traveling, Tubman arrived in Philadelphia, Pennsylvania. She stood in awe. It was as if she had crossed an invisible line to a new world. Her courage had carried her to freedom at last.

The North Star, called Polaris, mostly stays in place when the Earth rotates. It is always in the north. This makes the star a helpful tool for people to find their way.

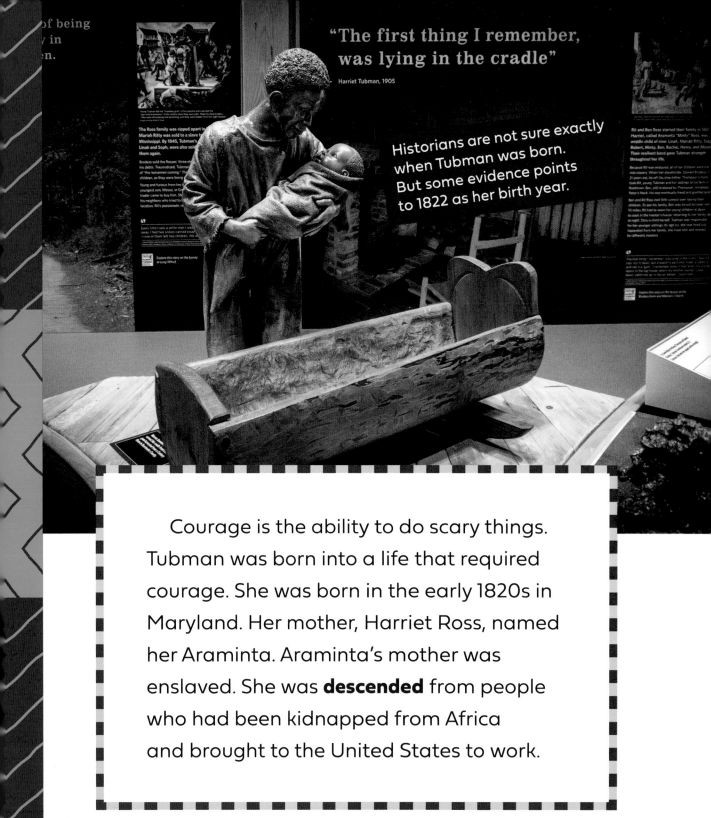

"The first thing I remember, was lying in the cradle"

Harriet Tubman, 1905

Historians are not sure exactly when Tubman was born. But some evidence points to 1822 as her birth year.

Courage is the ability to do scary things. Tubman was born into a life that required courage. She was born in the early 1820s in Maryland. Her mother, Harriet Ross, named her Araminta. Araminta's mother was enslaved. She was **descended** from people who had been kidnapped from Africa and brought to the United States to work.

Enslaved people were treated like property. They could be bought and sold. Their children were considered property, too. That meant that Araminta and her eight **siblings** were born into slavery.

Araminta's family worked on a farm in Bucktown, Maryland. Over the years, the family was split apart. Her father was forced to work far away. Her sisters were sold. But Araminta's mother fought hard to keep what remained of her family together. This courage inspired Araminta.

I never learned to write, so I found a woman to write my biography.

Araminta found her own courage when she was about 12. She saw another enslaved person try to escape. The enslaver called on Araminta to capture the freedom seeker. She refused. This was dangerous. But Araminta stood strong.

The enslaver was enraged. He threw a heavy weight at the freedom seeker. He missed and hit Araminta's head. Her skull cracked. Araminta barely survived her injury. She had headaches and **seizures**. During the seizures, she saw visions of freedom. Her urge to be free grew.

Tubman was often called "the Moses of her people." Moses was a religious figure who is said to have led his people out of slavery in Egypt.

In 1844, Araminta married a man named John Tubman. He was not enslaved. Araminta changed her name to Harriet Tubman. She talked to her husband about running away. Slavery was illegal in the north. If they fled, she could be free. John refused. If Harriet were to run away, she would have to go without him.

Sculptor Wesley Wofford created a sculpture called Harriet Tubman: The Journey to Freedom.

In 1849, Tubman learned that she might be sold. She could be sent anywhere. Tubman decided it was time to escape.

When Tubman crossed into Philadelphia, it was as a free woman. Her dreams of escape had finally come true. But her own freedom was not enough. She thought of other enslaved people still in Maryland. She knew that she had to go back for them.

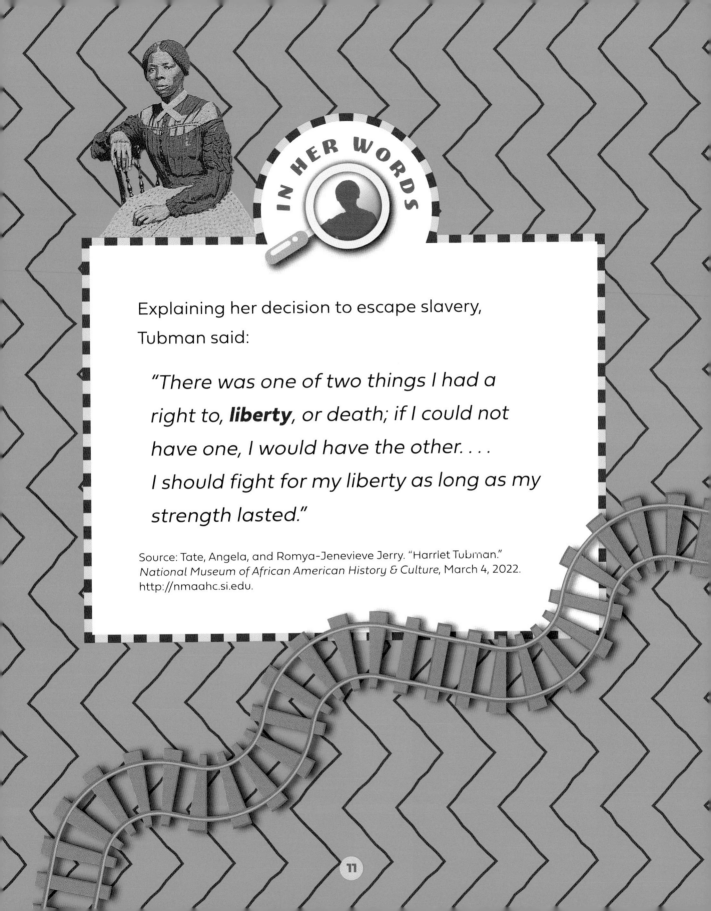

IN HER WORDS

Explaining her decision to escape slavery, Tubman said:

*"There was one of two things I had a right to, **liberty**, or death; if I could not have one, I would have the other. . . . I should fight for my liberty as long as my strength lasted."*

Source: Tate, Angela, and Romya-Jenevieve Jerry. "Harriet Tubman." *National Museum of African American History & Culture*, March 4, 2022. http://nmaahc.si.edu.

CONDUCTOR ON THE UNDERGROUND RAILROAD

Sometimes people have to do something hard or frightening. It takes courage to face these obstacles. People may be afraid. But courageous people do what is right anyway. It took courage for Tubman to escape enslavement. But her courageous journey did not end when she reached Pennsylvania. She was just getting started.

Tubman had not made it to Pennsylvania on her own. People had helped her along the way. Some had let her stay in their homes. Others had given her rides in carts.

The Harriet Tubman Underground Railroad Historic Park in Maryland teaches visitors about Tubman and her work on the Underground Railroad.

These people were part of a network called the Underground Railroad. This network was made up of abolitionists (a-buh-LIH-shun-ists). These were people who believed slavery was wrong. They courageously worked together to help enslaved people escape. Some led enslaved people to freedom. These people were called *conductors*. Others gave freedom seekers places to hide. These people were called *station masters*.

Tubman wanted to go back to Maryland to rescue her friends and family. She decided to use the Underground Railroad. She would be their conductor to freedom.

In 1850, Tubman traveled back to Maryland to begin rescuing her loved ones. This took courage. The US government had passed a law called the Fugitive Slave Act. This law made it illegal to help freedom seekers escape. If Tubman went back for her friends, she would be committing a crime. The law said anyone who saw her must bring her back to her enslaver. But Tubman did not let the law stop her from doing what was right.

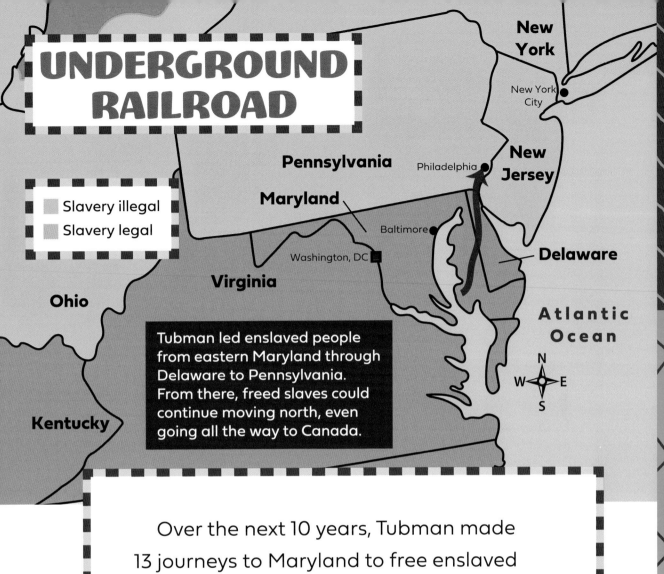

UNDERGROUND RAILROAD

New York

New York City

Pennsylvania

Philadelphia

New Jersey

Maryland

Slavery illegal
Slavery legal

Baltimore

Delaware

Washington, DC

Virginia

Ohio

Atlantic Ocean

N
W E
S

Tubman led enslaved people from eastern Maryland through Delaware to Pennsylvania. From there, freed slaves could continue moving north, even going all the way to Canada.

Kentucky

Over the next 10 years, Tubman made 13 journeys to Maryland to free enslaved people. She helped more than 70 people escape north. These people included her friends, parents, and brothers. She gave instructions to another 70 enslaved people who escaped on their own. She said that throughout her dangerous missions, she never lost a single person.

CHAPTER 3

LIFE AND LEGACY

In 1861, everything changed. The US Civil War (1861–1865) began. The North and South went to war over many issues. A big one was whether slavery should be legal. Hundreds of thousands of people died in the war. Tubman gathered her courage and volunteered to help. She enlisted as a nurse for the Union, the northern army. But soon she found a new opportunity. Tubman decided to become a spy.

In 1863, Tubman's work as a spy began. She was the perfect person for the job. She had spent years sneaking people to freedom. She knew how to remain undiscovered.

Tubman was the first woman in the United States to lead a military raid.

UNION NURSE
Tubman was a talented nurse. She used native plants to make medicines to help sick soldiers. She courageously tended to dying patients, even when it put her at risk of becoming ill.

17

Tubman led a group of spies through eastern South Carolina. They mapped the area. They also invited enslaved people to join the Union Army. All the while, Tubman was planning her biggest rescue mission yet.

On June 1, Tubman boarded a ship. She was leading 300 Black soldiers up the Combahee River. They stopped at Nichols **Plantation**. The soldiers stormed the plantation. They burned buildings down and took food. Then, they rescued the enslaved people forced to work on the plantation. The soldiers rescued 750 people. Many of the men went on to join the Union Army. Today, the mission is known as the Combahee Ferry Raid. It was so successful that the Union repeated the mission at other plantations. Tubman's courage saved hundreds of lives.

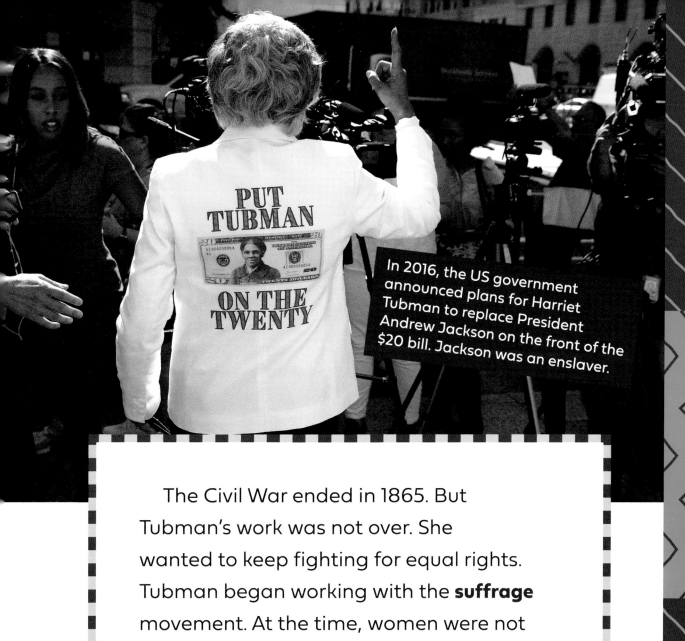

In 2016, the US government announced plans for Harriet Tubman to replace President Andrew Jackson on the front of the $20 bill. Jackson was an enslaver.

The Civil War ended in 1865. But Tubman's work was not over. She wanted to keep fighting for equal rights. Tubman began working with the **suffrage** movement. At the time, women were not allowed to vote. The suffrage movement wanted to change that. It takes courage to fight against **discrimination**. But Tubman had plenty of courage.

(From left) Tubman, Gertie, Davis, and other family and friends posed for a photo at Tubman's Auburn, New York, home.

In 1869, Tubman married a man named Nelson Davis. They adopted a daughter named Gertie. In 1896, Tubman founded a home for elderly and disabled Black people in Auburn, New York. Eventually, Tubman moved into the home. She passed away in the home in 1913.

Tubman's courage continues to inspire people today. Her bravery in the face of danger reminds others to have courage. More than a hundred years after her death, she is remembered as a hero.

WONDER MORE

Wondering About New Information
How much did you know about courage and Harriet Tubman before reading this book? What new information did you learn? Write down three new facts that this book taught you. Was the new information surprising? Why or why not?

Wondering How It Matters
What role does courage play in your life? Is there a time when you have acted with courage? How do you think the people around you have shown courage?

Wondering Why
Tubman showed courage by returning to Maryland even though she could have been enslaved again. Why do you think courage was important to Tubman? Is courage important to you?

Ways to Keep Wondering
Courage is a complex topic. After reading this book, what questions do you have about it? What can you do to learn more about courage?

FAST FACTS

- Courage is the ability to do things that are scary. Araminta Ross was born in the early 1820s in Maryland. She was born into slavery. It took courage to survive.

- After getting married, Araminta changed her name to Harriet Tubman. In 1849, Tubman fled north to Pennsylvania, where slavery was illegal. She could have been hurt or killed if she had been caught.

- Tubman made 13 trips south to bring enslaved friends and family members to freedom. She put the lives of others ahead of her own safety.

- During the Civil War, Tubman showed courage by serving as a nurse and a spy. She helped free 750 people in a military raid.

- Tubman did not let discrimination stop her. After the Civil War, Tubman fought for equal rights for women.

BEING A LEADER

Tubman showed courage by being a leader. You can be a leader, too. What is a cause that you care about? Write down a few causes that matter to you. Choose one and tell your friends. Together, think of a few ways you can show support for your cause.

GLOSSARY

descended (dih-SEN-ded) People are descended from their older family members and people who lived long ago. Tubman was descended from people who had been kidnapped from Africa.

discrimination (diss-krim-ih-NAY-shun) Discrimination is the unfair treatment of others based on race, gender, or other traits. Tubman faced discrimination because she was Black.

liberty (LIH-ber-tee) Liberty is freedom. Tubman fought for the liberty of enslaved people.

plantation (plan-TAY-shun) A plantation is a big farm. Tubman freed 750 enslaved people from a plantation.

seizures (SEE-zhurz) Seizures are periods of unconsciousness that sometimes include physical effects such as shaking. After Tubman was hit with a heavy weight, she had seizures.

siblings (SIH-blings) Siblings are people who share a parent or parents, such as brothers and sisters. Tubman helped some of her siblings escape slavery.

suffrage (SUH-frij) Suffrage is the right to vote. Tubman fought for women's suffrage.

FIND OUT MORE

In the Library

Brown-Wood, JaNay. *Harriet Tubman.*
New York, NY: A Golden Book, 2022.

Kelly, Christa. *Bravery: The Story of Malala Yousafzai.* Parker, CO: The Child's World, 2026.

Troy, Don. *Harriet Ross Tubman: Abolitionist and Activist.* Parker, CO: The Child's World, 2024.

On the Web

Visit our website for links about
courage and Harriet Tubman:
childsworld.com/links

Note to Parents, Caregivers, Teachers, and Librarians: We routinely verify our web links to make sure they are safe and active sites. So encourage your readers to check them out!

INDEX